EMMANUEL JOSEPH

The Infinite Loop, History, Technology, and the Search for Meaning

Contents

1

Chapter 1: The Dawn of Humanity

In the beginning, humanity emerged from the shadows of prehistory, slowly evolving from primitive beings into conscious, thinking entities. The first sparks of ingenuity appeared as rudimentary tools and fire, altering the course of human history. As our ancestors tamed their environment, they laid the foundation for future civilizations. With each discovery, they transcended the limitations of their natural world, carving a path toward technological advancement.

The essence of humanity's early struggles centered on survival and adaptation. Nomadic tribes roamed vast landscapes, seeking sustenance and shelter. The invention of agriculture marked a turning point, allowing communities to settle and thrive. With stable food sources, populations grew, and complex societies began to form. The rhythm of life, once dictated by the elements, now followed the cycles of planting and harvest.

As settlements expanded, so too did the exchange of ideas and knowledge. The development of language and written symbols enabled the preservation and transmission of cultural heritage. Early societies built monuments and structures, leaving behind traces of their existence. These ancient relics offer glimpses into the past, revealing the ingenuity and creativity of our ancestors.

In this dawn of humanity, the seeds of technological progress were sown. The journey from stone tools to advanced machinery was set in motion, driven by curiosity and the relentless pursuit of improvement. This unyielding spirit of innovation would continue to shape the course of history, guiding humanity through the ages.

2

Chapter 2: The Rise of Civilizations

With the advent of agriculture, humanity transitioned from nomadic lifestyles to settled communities. The rise of early civilizations marked a new era of social, cultural, and technological development. Mesopotamia, often hailed as the cradle of civilization, witnessed the birth of complex societies, intricate systems of governance, and monumental architecture. The Sumerians, Akkadians, Babylonians, and Assyrians each left indelible marks on history, showcasing the power of human ingenuity.

As civilizations flourished, so too did the exchange of ideas and knowledge. Trade routes connected distant lands, fostering cultural exchanges and the dissemination of technological advancements. The Phoenicians, renowned for their maritime prowess, created a network of trade that spanned the Mediterranean. Their development of a phonetic alphabet revolutionized written communication, paving the way for future languages and literary traditions.

In the realm of science and mathematics, ancient civilizations made significant strides. The Egyptians, with their advanced understanding of geometry and engineering, constructed awe-inspiring structures such as the pyramids. The Greeks, led by thinkers like Pythagoras, Euclid, and Archimedes, laid the groundwork for modern scientific principles. Their pursuit of knowledge extended to philosophy, literature, and the arts, enriching human culture and intellectual pursuits.

The rise of civilizations also saw the emergence of powerful empires that shaped the course of history. The Roman Empire, with its vast territories and sophisticated infrastructure, left a lasting legacy on Western civilization. The Chinese dynasties, including the Qin and Han, made groundbreaking advancements in technology, governance, and culture. These early civilizations, each with their unique contributions, set the stage for the future development of humanity.

3

Chapter 3: The Age of Discovery

The Age of Discovery ushered in a period of exploration and expansion, driven by a thirst for knowledge and adventure. European nations embarked on voyages across uncharted waters, seeking new trade routes and territories. The exploits of explorers such as Christopher Columbus, Ferdinand Magellan, and Vasco da Gama reshaped the global map and opened new horizons for humanity.

The discoveries made during this era had profound implications for science, technology, and culture. The exchange of goods, ideas, and knowledge between continents led to unprecedented advancements in various fields. The introduction of new crops, such as potatoes, tomatoes, and maize, transformed agricultural practices and diets worldwide. The spread of scientific knowledge accelerated, with figures like Galileo Galilei, Johannes Kepler, and Isaac Newton revolutionizing our understanding of the natural world.

The Age of Discovery also brought about the rise of colonial empires, with European powers establishing control over vast territories. The economic and political motivations behind colonization led to the exploitation of resources and indigenous populations. The consequences of these actions continue to reverberate through history, shaping the modern world and influencing contemporary discussions on social justice and equality.

Despite the darker aspects of this period, the spirit of exploration and discovery remained a driving force behind human progress. The advancements made during the Age of Discovery laid the groundwork for future innovations and the continued quest for knowledge. As humanity ventured into new frontiers, the pursuit of understanding and meaning became an integral part of our shared journey.

4

Chapter 4: The Industrial Revolution

The Industrial Revolution marked a seismic shift in human history, transforming economies, societies, and technologies. Emerging in the late 18th century, this era saw the rise of mechanization and mass production. Innovations such as the steam engine, the spinning jenny, and the power loom revolutionized industries, increasing efficiency and productivity. Factories sprang up, drawing people from rural areas to urban centers in search of work and opportunity.

The impact of the Industrial Revolution extended beyond economic changes. It altered the very fabric of society, reshaping social structures and labor dynamics. The rise of a new working class, coupled with the growth of a wealthy industrial bourgeoisie, created tensions and conflicts. Workers faced grueling conditions, long hours, and meager wages, leading to the formation of labor unions and movements advocating for better rights and protections.

Technological advancements during this period were not confined to industry alone. The revolution in transportation, with the advent of railways and steamships, connected distant regions and facilitated the movement of goods and people. Communication also underwent a transformation, with the invention of the telegraph enabling instant transmission of information across vast distances. These innovations laid the groundwork for the interconnected world we live in today.

The Industrial Revolution was a testament to humanity's capacity for innovation and adaptation. It demonstrated the power of technology to drive progress and shape the course of history. However, it also highlighted the need for balance and consideration of the social and environmental impacts of rapid technological change. As we continue to navigate the complexities of the modern world, the lessons of the Industrial Revolution remain ever-relevant.

5

Chapter 5: The Digital Age

The latter half of the 20th century witnessed the dawn of the Digital Age, a period defined by the rapid development and proliferation of information technology. The invention of the transistor in the 1940s paved the way for the creation of computers, which evolved from room-sized machines to compact personal devices. The emergence of the internet in the late 20th century revolutionized communication, enabling instant access to information and connecting people across the globe.

The Digital Age brought about unprecedented changes in various aspects of life. In the realm of business, the rise of e-commerce transformed traditional retail models, allowing consumers to shop online from the comfort of their homes. The advent of social media platforms redefined how people interact and share information, creating virtual communities and amplifying voices. These technological advancements also facilitated the growth of the gig economy, offering new opportunities and challenges for the workforce.

Education and entertainment were equally impacted by the digital revolution. Online learning platforms provided access to knowledge and skills for individuals worldwide, breaking down geographical barriers. The entertainment industry saw a shift towards digital content, with streaming services offering on-demand access to movies, music, and television shows. Virtual reality and augmented reality technologies further expanded the possibilities for immersive experiences.

While the Digital Age has brought about remarkable progress, it has also raised important questions about privacy, security, and the ethical implications of technology. The proliferation of data and the rise of artificial intelligence have sparked debates on the balance between innovation and regulation. As we navigate this new era, the search for meaning and purpose in an increasingly digital world continues to shape our collective journey.

6

Chapter 6: The Quest for Meaning

Throughout history, humanity has sought to understand the deeper meaning of existence. This quest has taken many forms, from religious and philosophical inquiries to artistic and scientific explorations. Each era has offered its unique perspectives and interpretations, reflecting the evolving understanding of the human condition.

Religious traditions have long provided frameworks for understanding the mysteries of life and the universe. Ancient belief systems, such as those of the Egyptians, Greeks, and Hindus, offered explanations for natural phenomena and guidance for living a virtuous life. The emergence of monotheistic religions, including Judaism, Christianity, and Islam, introduced new theological concepts and ethical principles that continue to influence millions of people worldwide.

Philosophical thought has also played a crucial role in the search for meaning. Thinkers like Socrates, Plato, and Aristotle explored fundamental questions about existence, knowledge, and ethics. Their ideas laid the foundation for Western philosophy and inspired subsequent generations of scholars and intellectuals. In the East, philosophies such as Confucianism, Taoism, and Buddhism offered alternative perspectives on the nature of reality and the path to enlightenment.

Art and literature have provided another avenue for exploring the human experience. Through storytelling, music, and visual expression, artists have sought to capture the essence of emotions, dreams, and aspirations. Great works of art and literature, from the epics of Homer to the plays of Shakespeare, have resonated across time and cultures, offering insights into the complexities of the human soul.

In the modern era, science and technology have added new dimensions to the quest for meaning. Advances in fields such as astronomy, biology, and neuroscience have expanded our understanding of the universe and the mechanisms of life. The exploration of space, the decoding of the human genome, and the study of consciousness have opened new frontiers for inquiry and discovery. Yet, even as we uncover the secrets of the cosmos, the search for meaning remains an intrinsic part of the human journey.

7

Chapter 7: The Human Condition

The human condition is characterized by a quest for understanding, purpose, and connection. Throughout history, individuals have grappled with existential questions, seeking to find meaning in the midst of life's joys and challenges. This search for meaning has been a driving force behind human creativity, resilience, and innovation.

At the core of the human condition is the desire for connection. People seek relationships and communities that provide a sense of belonging and support. Love, friendship, and family are central to the human experience, offering solace and joy. The bonds formed through these connections create a tapestry of shared experiences and memories, enriching the lives of individuals and communities.

The pursuit of meaning also involves navigating the complexities of identity and self-discovery. People strive to understand their own values, beliefs, and aspirations, often reflecting on their past experiences and envisioning their future. This journey of self-discovery is a continuous process, shaped by personal growth and the evolving understanding of one's place in the world.

Art, literature, and philosophy have long been avenues for exploring the human condition. Through creative expression, individuals can delve into the depths of their emotions and experiences, shedding light on the intricacies of the human soul. The stories, music, and visual art that emerge from this exploration resonate with others, fostering empathy and a deeper understanding of the shared human experience.

8

Chapter 8: The Intersection of History and Technology

History and technology are deeply intertwined, with each influencing the development and trajectory of the other. Technological advancements have played a crucial role in shaping the course of history, driving societal changes and enabling new forms of communication and interaction. Conversely, historical events and cultural shifts have spurred technological innovation, as societies seek solutions to emerging challenges.

Throughout history, key technological breakthroughs have marked significant turning points. The invention of the printing press in the 15th century revolutionized the dissemination of knowledge, making books and written materials more accessible to the masses. This democratization of information paved the way for the spread of ideas and the rise of the Enlightenment, a period marked by intellectual and scientific advancements.

The development of the steam engine during the Industrial Revolution transformed industries and transportation, ushering in an era of unprecedented economic growth and urbanization. The rise of the internet in the late 20th century connected people across the globe, facilitating the exchange of information and fostering new forms of collaboration. These technological milestones have shaped the modern world, influencing how we live, work, and communicate.

As we navigate the complexities of the Digital Age, the intersection of history and technology continues to evolve. The advancements in artificial intelligence, biotechnology, and renewable energy hold the potential to address pressing global challenges, from climate change to healthcare. Understanding the historical context of these developments provides valuable insights into their implications and ethical considerations, guiding us towards a more sustainable and equitable future.

9

Chapter 9: The Role of Science in the Search for Meaning

Science has been a powerful tool in humanity's quest for understanding and meaning. Through systematic observation and experimentation, scientists have unraveled the mysteries of the natural world, shedding light on the underlying principles that govern the universe. This pursuit of knowledge has expanded our horizons, revealing the intricate complexity and beauty of the cosmos.

The scientific method, rooted in empirical evidence and rational inquiry, has driven countless discoveries and innovations. From the laws of physics to the principles of biology, science has provided a framework for understanding the fundamental workings of nature. Breakthroughs in fields such as astronomy, chemistry, and medicine have transformed our lives, improving health and well-being, and expanding our understanding of the universe.

However, the role of science in the search for meaning extends beyond practical applications. Science fosters a sense of wonder and curiosity, encouraging us to explore the unknown and question our assumptions. The awe-inspiring discoveries made through scientific inquiry, from the vastness of space to the intricacies of the human genome, inspire a profound appreciation for the complexity and interconnectedness of life.

Moreover, science serves as a bridge between different cultures and perspectives, fostering collaboration and mutual understanding. The global nature of scientific research transcends national and cultural boundaries, uniting people in the shared pursuit of knowledge. This spirit of cooperation and curiosity reflects the universal human desire to comprehend the world and find meaning in our existence.

10

Chapter 10: The Role of Technology in Human Connection

Technology has revolutionized the way we connect with one another, bridging gaps and fostering global communities. From the invention of the telegraph and telephone to the rise of social media and video conferencing, technological advancements have redefined communication. These innovations have transformed personal relationships, business interactions, and cultural exchanges, creating a more interconnected world.

The internet, in particular, has played a pivotal role in facilitating human connection. Social media platforms enable people to stay in touch with friends and family, share experiences, and engage in discussions regardless of geographic distances. Online communities bring together individuals with shared interests, providing a sense of belonging and support. The digital age has also given rise to virtual friendships and collaborations, transcending the limitations of physical proximity.

In the realm of business, technology has enabled seamless communication and collaboration across borders. Video conferencing tools allow teams to work together in real time, regardless of location. Remote work has become increasingly prevalent, offering flexibility and new opportunities for professionals. E-commerce platforms have transformed the way we shop, connecting consumers with products and services from around the world.

However, the proliferation of digital communication also presents challenges. The reliance on technology can lead to issues such as digital addiction, social isolation, and concerns about privacy and security. It is essential to strike a balance between the benefits of technology and the need for meaningful, in-person connections. As we navigate the digital landscape, the search for authentic and fulfilling relationships remains a central aspect of the human experience.

11

Chapter 11: The Ethics of Technological Advancement

The rapid pace of technological advancement raises important ethical considerations. As we develop and deploy new technologies, it is crucial to reflect on their potential impact on society, the environment, and individual well-being. Ethical frameworks provide guidance on how to navigate these complexities, ensuring that technology serves the greater good and aligns with our values.

One of the key ethical issues in technology is the question of privacy. The collection and use of personal data by companies and governments have sparked debates about consent, surveillance, and data security. Ensuring that individuals have control over their personal information and protecting their privacy is a fundamental ethical concern in the digital age.

Artificial intelligence (AI) presents another set of ethical challenges. The development of AI technologies raises questions about bias, accountability, and the potential for unintended consequences. It is essential to address issues such as algorithmic fairness, transparency, and the responsible use of AI in decision-making processes. Ethical considerations must also guide the development of autonomous systems, ensuring that they align with human values and priorities.

Environmental sustainability is another critical ethical consideration in technology. The production and disposal of electronic devices contribute to environmental degradation and resource depletion. It is important to adopt practices that minimize the environmental impact of technology, such as recycling, energy-efficient design, and the use of sustainable materials. Ethical frameworks can help guide the development and deployment of technologies that support a more sustainable future.

12

Chapter 12: The Future of Technology

As we look to the future, technology holds the promise of transforming our lives in ways we can only imagine. Emerging fields such as artificial intelligence, quantum computing, and biotechnology have the potential to revolutionize industries, improve health outcomes, and address global challenges. However, the future of technology also brings uncertainties and risks that require careful consideration.

Artificial intelligence is poised to become increasingly integrated into various aspects of life, from healthcare and education to transportation and entertainment. AI-powered systems have the potential to enhance productivity, provide personalized services, and drive innovation. However, it is essential to ensure that AI technologies are developed and used responsibly, with a focus on fairness, transparency, and accountability.

Quantum computing represents another frontier in technological advancement. This emerging field has the potential to revolutionize computing by solving complex problems that are currently beyond the reach of classical computers. Quantum computers could enable breakthroughs in fields such as cryptography, material science, and drug discovery. However, the development and implementation of quantum technologies also raise ethical and security concerns that must be addressed.

Biotechnology and genetic engineering hold promise for improving health and extending human lifespan. Advances in fields such as gene editing and regenerative medicine have the potential to cure diseases and enhance human capabilities. However, these technologies also raise ethical questions about the boundaries of human enhancement and the potential for unintended consequences.

13

Chapter 13: The Search for Meaning in a Technological World

In an increasingly technological world, the search for meaning remains a fundamental aspect of the human experience. While technology can enhance our lives and expand our horizons, it is essential to cultivate a sense of purpose and connection that transcends the digital realm. This search for meaning involves reflecting on our values, relationships, and aspirations, and finding ways to lead fulfilling and meaningful lives.

One way to find meaning is through the pursuit of knowledge and personal growth. Lifelong learning, curiosity, and a passion for discovery can enrich our lives and provide a sense of purpose. Engaging with diverse perspectives, exploring new interests, and challenging ourselves to grow intellectually and emotionally can foster a deeper understanding of ourselves and the world around us.

Another avenue for finding meaning is through relationships and community. Building and nurturing meaningful connections with others can provide a sense of belonging and support. Acts of kindness, empathy, and compassion can strengthen our bonds and create a positive impact on those around us. Community engagement, whether through volunteering, activism, or social initiatives, allows us to contribute to the greater good and find purpose in serving others.

Creative expression is also a powerful way to explore and communicate meaning. Whether through art, music, writing, or other forms of creativity, expressing our thoughts, emotions, and experiences can help us connect with others and understand ourselves better. Creative endeavors can provide a sense of fulfillment and joy, offering an outlet for self-expression and exploration.

14

Chapter 14: Balancing Technology and Humanity

As technology continues to evolve, it is crucial to strike a balance between technological advancement and the essence of our humanity. While technology can enhance our lives in countless ways, it is essential to ensure that it does not overshadow the core values that define us as human beings. This balance requires mindful consideration of how we integrate technology into our daily lives and society at large.

One important aspect of this balance is the need to maintain genuine human connections. While digital communication offers convenience and accessibility, it is important to prioritize face-to-face interactions and meaningful relationships. Taking the time to engage in real-world experiences, whether through shared activities, conversations, or community involvement, helps foster a sense of belonging and emotional well-being.

Additionally, it is essential to be mindful of the impact of technology on our mental and physical health. The constant connectivity and information overload associated with digital devices can lead to stress, anxiety, and burnout. Practicing digital mindfulness, setting boundaries for screen time, and engaging in activities that promote relaxation and self-care can help mitigate these effects and promote a healthier relationship with technology.

Education and awareness play a critical role in achieving this balance. By fostering a deeper understanding of the ethical implications of technology and promoting digital literacy, individuals can make informed choices about how they use and interact with technology. Encouraging critical thinking, empathy, and responsible behavior in the digital realm can help create a more compassionate and thoughtful society.

15

Chapter 15: The Infinite Loop

The infinite loop represents the continuous and cyclical nature of history, technology, and the search for meaning. As humanity progresses, we encounter recurring themes and challenges that shape our journey. Each new era brings technological advancements that redefine our understanding of the world and our place within it. At the same time, the quest for meaning remains a constant, guiding us through the complexities of life.

Throughout history, humanity has demonstrated an unwavering spirit of curiosity and innovation. From the earliest civilizations to the present day, our collective efforts have driven progress and shaped the course of history. This relentless pursuit of knowledge and improvement has led to remarkable achievements, but it has also highlighted the need for balance, reflection, and ethical consideration.

The infinite loop also symbolizes the interconnectedness of all aspects of life. History, technology, and the search for meaning are not separate entities but are intertwined, influencing and shaping one another. As we navigate this intricate web, it is essential to recognize the impact of our actions and decisions on the broader context of humanity and the environment.

In the end, the search for meaning is a deeply personal and universal journey. It is a quest that transcends time, culture, and technology, reflecting the essence of what it means to be human. As we move forward, embracing the lessons of the past and the possibilities of the future, we continue to explore the infinite loop, seeking to understand, connect, and find purpose in our existence.

The Infinite Loop: History, Technology, and the Search for Meaning

In "The Infinite Loop: History, Technology, and the Search for Meaning," explore the ever-evolving relationship between humanity, technology, and the quest for understanding. This captivating narrative traces the arc of human history, from the dawn of civilization through the Industrial Revolution and into the Digital Age. Each chapter unravels the intricate tapestry of technological advancements and their profound impact on societies and cultures.

Delve into the triumphs and challenges that have defined our journey, from early tools and agriculture to the rise of artificial intelligence and quantum computing. Alongside these technological milestones, the book examines humanity's enduring search for meaning—through religion, philosophy, art, and science—revealing how our quest for purpose shapes and is shaped by the technologies we create.

Through compelling stories and insightful analysis, "The Infinite Loop" invites readers to reflect on the interconnectedness of history, technology, and human experience. It underscores the importance of balancing innovation with ethical considerations and the need to maintain our humanity in an increasingly digital world. This thought-provoking exploration offers a deeper understanding of our past, present, and future, guiding us in the pursuit of a more meaningful and connected existence.